soups

soups

ELSA PETERSEN-SCHEPELERN
with photography by Jeremy Hopley

RYLAND
PETERS
& SMALL

LONDON NEW YORK

R Y L A N D

P E T E R S

& S M A L L

LONDON NEW YORK

First published in the United States in 1999 as *Blended Soups*.
This edition published 2002
by Ryland Peters & Small, Inc.
519 Broadway, 5th Floor
New York, NY 10012
www.rylandpeters.com

10 9 8 7 6 5 4 3 2 1

Printed in China

Library of Congress Cataloging-in-Publication Data

Petersen-Schepelern, Elsa.
  Soups / by Elsa Petersen-Schepelern.
    p. cm.
  Includes index.
  ISBN 1-84172-361-4
  1. Soups 2. Blenders (Cookery) I. Title.

TX757 .P463 2002
641.8'13--dc21   2002024853

Publishing Director	Anne Ryland
Head of Design	Gabriella Le Grazie
Designer	Ashley Western
Design Assistant	Sailesh Patel
Editorial Assistant	Maddalena Bastianelli
Production	Patricia Harrington
Food Stylists	Elsa Petersen-Schepelern, Fiona Smith
Stylist	Wei Tang
Photographer's Assistant	Karen Thomas
Author Photograph	Francis Loney

Acknowledgments

My thanks to my nephew Luc Votan for his expert advice, to my sister
Kirsten and to Fiona Smith for her guiding hand with food styling.

Notes

All spoon measurements are level unless otherwise noted.
Raw or partly cooked eggs should not be served to the very young, the old,
the frail, or to pregnant women.
Specialty Asian ingredients are available in large supermarkets, Thai,
Chinese, Japanese and Vietnamese stores, as well as Asian stores.

contents

INTRODUCTION

What did we do before the invention of blenders, food processors, spice grinders, and their ilk? A lot of hard work, that's what!

These kitchen appliances are especially useful in making soups—turning vegetables into creamy purées, beans into a crunchy mixture, spices into powders or pastes, meat and poultry into delicious fillings for wontons and dumplings. The soups in this book are suitable for quick meals at home or for grander occasions such as dinner parties. I've even served them in mini-quantities at parties. They're so fast and easy, I don't know why people bother buying ready-made ones full of preservatives!

Homemade Stocks

You must have good stock, either homemade or bought from the supermarket. Being the world's laziest cook, I make mine in a microwave: it's quick, easy, and clearer than the traditional kind. Put crushed parsley stalks, 1 onion, 1 carrot, and 1 celery stalk, all chopped, in a microwave-safe dish. Add 1 lb. chicken pieces such as wings, or meat bones and trimmings, fill with boiling water, cover and microwave on HIGH (750 watt oven) for 35 minutes. Let stand for 30 minutes, then strain off the liquid and discard the solids. Cool at room temperature until the fat rises to the surface, then chill. Remove and discard the fat, then use the stock within 1–2 days or freeze. (Strain at least 4 times through cheesecloth for a clearer stock.) For vegetable stock, use extra vegetables instead of chicken. Microwave on HIGH for 20 minutes, then let stand for 20 minutes.

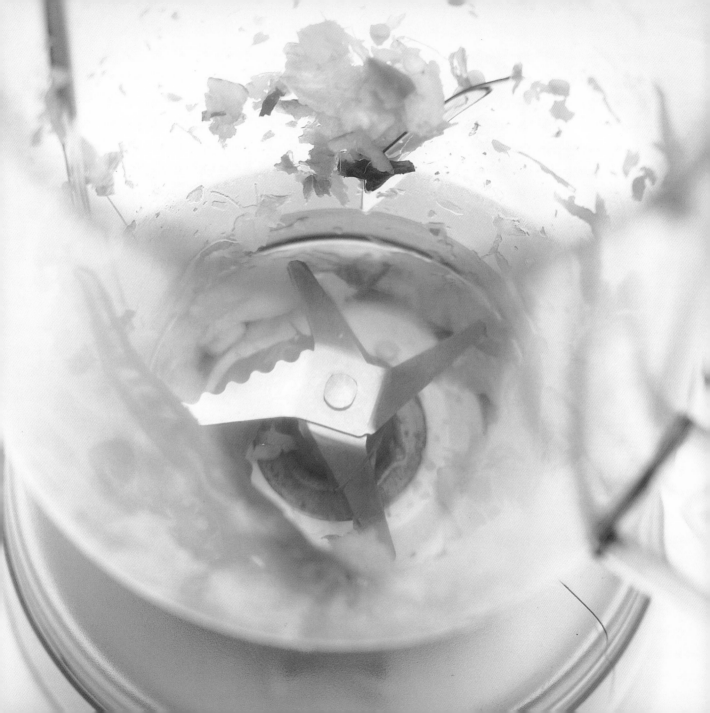

Peel and core the peppers with a vegetable peeler and chop the flesh into a blender. Add the yellow tomatoes and garlic and blend to a purée. Add the stock and 1 cup crushed ice and blend again. Add salt and pepper, then chill until very cold. Using a mandoline or very sharp knife, slice the cucumber and radishes paper-thin.

Pour the purée into a glass soup tureen or separate bowls or glasses, adding extra ice if preferred. Top with the cucumbers, radishes, scallions, and red cherry tomatoes. Serve, sprinkled with the herbs, salt, and cracked black pepper.

yellow gazpacho

4 yellow or orange bell peppers

1 basket yellow cherry tomatoes, halved

2 garlic cloves, crushed with salt

3 cups chicken or vegetable stock

1 mini cucumber, halved lengthwise
  and seeded

6 radishes

4 scallions, sliced

4 red cherry tomatoes, quartered

a few sprigs of parsley, chopped

a handful of chives, snipped (optional)

small sprigs of mint or basil

salt and cracked black pepper, to taste

serves 4–6

I'm not usually a fan of gazpacho, because the blended kind sometimes looks decidedly khaki. This one is a colorful exception, with clear, bright tastes. I think peppers are vastly improved when peeled, so use a vegetable peeler before coring.

coconut vichyssoise

I'm a fan of vichyssoise—and of coconut—and thought it was an inspired idea to put the two together. I prefer this soup hot or warm rather than cold, but please yourself.

Melt the butter and oil in a saucepan, add the onion and leeks, and sauté gently until softened and translucent.

Add the potatoes, stock, and salt and simmer until the potatoes are soft, about 20 minutes. Transfer to a blender and purée until smooth. Add the coconut milk and enough extra stock to produce a thick, creamy consistency. Reheat if necessary, then serve hot or warm, with a trail of cream on top and your choice of other toppings, such as fresh chives or toasted fresh coconut.

1 tablespoon butter

1 tablespoon corn or sunflower oil

1 onion, finely sliced

3 leeks, white only, sliced

2 large potatoes, sliced

1 cup chicken or vegetable stock, plus extra (see method)

a pinch of sea salt

1 cup canned coconut milk

To serve, your choice of:

¼ cup light cream

chives or Chinese chives, snipped

slivers of fresh coconut, lightly toasted

serves 4

carrot and ginger soup

with limes and clementines

Grated zest of limes and clementines give a certain spark to this golden gingery soup. I like the mild taste of clementine juice, but orange, mandarin, or tangerine juice would also be good.

2 tablespoons butter

2 tablespoons sunflower oil

2 onions, chopped

1 inch fresh ginger, finely chopped

1 lb. carrots (about 4–6), finely sliced

4 cups chicken stock or water

juice of 5 clementines (about ¾ cup)

sea salt and freshly ground black pepper

shreds of lime and clementine zest, to serve

serves 4

Heat the butter and oil in a saucepan, add the onions and a pinch of salt, and cook until softened and golden. Add the ginger and carrots and sauté a few minutes more. Add the stock or water, the clementine juice, salt, and pepper. Bring to a boil, then simmer until the carrots are tender, about 20 minutes.

Strain into a pitcher; put the solids into a blender with 1–2 ladles of strained liquid, then purée, adding extra liquid if necessary. When smooth, add the remaining liquid and purée again.

Reheat if necessary, taste and adjust the seasoning, then serve the soup in bowls and top with lime and clementine zest.

fresh tomato soup with lemon and basil

My sister in Australia grows the world's most wonderful tomatoes. This recipe is based on her delicious bottled tomatoes, though unfortunately my store-bought fruit can't compete with hers!

2 lb. very ripe red tomatoes

2 cups flavorful chicken stock

sea salt and coarsely crushed black pepper

juice and shredded zest of 1 lemon

¼ cup pesto (optional)

a bunch of chives, snipped, or basil

serves 4

To skin the tomatoes, cut a cross in the base of each, put in a bowl and cover with boiling water. Remove after 10 seconds and put into a strainer set over a large saucepan. Slip off and discard the skins and cut the tomatoes in half. Using a teaspoon, scrape the seed section into the strainer and put the flesh into the blender. Press the juice through the strainer and add to the blender, discarding the seeds.

Purée the tomatoes, adding a little of the stock to help the process. Add the remaining stock, season to taste, and transfer to the saucepan. Heat well without boiling (to keep the fresh flavor).

Serve in heated soup plates with a spoonful of lemon juice, lemon zest, pesto if using, chives or basil, and black pepper.

beet soup with lemon zest

Put the chopped beets into a blender, add 2 ladles stock, and purée until smooth. Add the remaining stock and purée again. Test for thickness and seasoning, adding extra stock or water if the purée is too thick. Blend again.

Serve hot or chilled, topped with your choice of sour cream or light cream, beet strips, and grated lemon zest.

5 cooked beets, 4 coarsely chopped
   and 1 sliced into fine strips
3 cups chicken or vegetable stock
sea salt and freshly ground black pepper

To serve (optional):
¼ cup sour cream or light cream
grated lemon zest

serves 4

chilled cucumber cream

Using a teaspoon, scrape the seeds out of the cucumbers and discard. Chop the flesh and skins coarsely, then transfer to a blender or food processor. Add the yogurt, dried mint, garlic, and crushed ice and blend to a green-flecked purée.

Taste and adjust the seasoning, then serve in chilled soup plates, topped with sprigs of mint.

4 mini cucumbers or 1 large cucumber
   (about 1 lb.), halved lengthwise
2 lb. plain yogurt (4 cups)
3 tablespoons dried mint
1 fat garlic clove, crushed
½ cup crushed ice
sea salt and coarsely crushed black pepper
sprigs of mint, to serve

serves 4

The blended element of this soup is *pistou*, the Provençal version of pesto. You need a big bunch of scented summertime basil.

soupe au pistou

Pistou:

leaves from 1 large bunch basil

2 garlic cloves, crushed

¼ cup freshly grated Parmesan cheese

olive oil (see method)

Soup:

1 red onion, cut into wedges

1 potato, diced

a handful of soup pasta, such as ditalini

4 cups clear chicken or vegetable stock*

salt and freshly ground black pepper

1 cup cooked or canned cannellini beans

Your choice of:

4 baby carrots, halved lengthwise

4 Brussels sprouts, halved

4 baby zucchini, halved lengthwise

1 red bell pepper, peeled, cored, and sliced

a handful of green peas

a handful of shelled fava beans

2 flat or runner beans, cut in short lengths

serves 4

To make the pistou, put the basil, garlic, and Parmesan in a blender or food processor and blend as finely as possible. Add enough olive oil in a steady stream to form a loose paste. Set aside.

Heat 1 tablespoon olive oil in a small skillet, add the onion, and sauté on both sides until softened. Cook the potato and soup pasta in boiling salted water until tender. Drain. Blanch your choice of carrots, sprouts, zucchini, pepper, peas, fava beans, flat or runner beans in boiling salted water until tender but crisp, 3–5 minutes. Drain and refresh in cold water. Pop the fava beans out of their gray skins and discard the skins.

Bring the stock to a boil, add seasoning, the cooked potato and pasta, and all the vegetables including the cannellini beans. Simmer for 2 minutes or until heated through. Serve in heated soup plates, with a separate bowl of pistou. Guests stir the pistou into their soup to taste.

Note: For a clear stock, strain it at least 4 times through cheesecloth.

1 onion, finely chopped

2 garlic cloves, crushed

1 inch fresh ginger, finely chopped

2 stalks lemongrass, finely chopped

2 red chilies, sliced, plus extra to serve

3 limes, 1 juiced, 2 cut into wedges

3 tablespoons peanut oil

1 lb. sweet potatoes (about 2 large), cut into large chunks

about 2 cups canned coconut milk

2 cups chicken stock

sea salt and freshly ground black pepper

serves 4

sweet potato soup

To make the spice paste, put the onion, garlic, ginger, lemongrass, chilies, lime juice, and half the oil in a blender and purée until smooth (add a little water if necessary).

Heat the remaining oil in a saucepan. Add the spice paste and stir-fry gently for 5 minutes. Add the sweet potatoes, coconut milk, and stock. Simmer until the sweet potatoes are soft.

Transfer to a blender, purée until smooth, season to taste, reheat if necessary, top with sliced chilies, and serve with wedges of lime.

roasted red pepper soup with arugula

Heat the oil in a skillet, add the onions and sauté gently until soft and golden. Push to the side of the pan, add the garlic and sauté for about 1 minute.

Meanwhile, halve and seed the peppers, put on a sheet of foil or a baking tray under a hot broiler, and cook until the skin is black and charred. Transfer to a bowl or saucepan and cover tightly with plastic wrap or a lid. Leave for about 10 minutes to steam, then transfer to a strainer set over the same bowl or pan. Scrape off and discard the skins (keep a few of the nice brown toasty bits if you like), putting the flesh back into the bowl or pan (catch as many of the toasted juices as possible).

Transfer to a blender, add the onions and garlic, and work to a purée, adding a little stock if necessary. Add the remaining stock and purée again, then transfer to a saucepan and heat to boiling point. Remove from the heat, season, then serve in heated soup plates.

Top with wild arugula, fresh thyme leaves, or small sprigs of oregano. For extra toasted flavor, add a few shards of toasted pepper skin to each bowl of soup.

Note: For relentless hotheads, a couple of medium-hot red chilies such as fresno or serrano may be broiled at the same time as the peppers and treated in the same way.

2 tablespoons olive oil

2 onions, halved and finely sliced

2 garlic cloves, crushed

8 long red bell peppers (or yellow or orange)

4 cups chicken or vegetable stock

sea salt and freshly ground black pepper

1 bunch wild arugula, thyme, or oregano

serves 4

japanese fresh corn soup

with scallions and tamari soy sauce

Bring a large saucepan of water to a boil, add the corn and simmer for about 15 minutes. Drain. Hold the cobs upright on a chopping board, blunt end down. Run a sharp knife down the cobs, shaving off the kernels.

Put the kernels into a blender with 1 cup stock. Purée until smooth, then press through a strainer into a saucepan. Return the corn to the blender, add another ladle of stock, purée, then strain as before, pushing through as much corn juice as possible. Repeat until as much juice as possible has been extracted. Reheat.

Put 1 egg yolk, if using, into each of 4 small soup bowls, ladle the soup on top, and beat with chopsticks (the hot soup cooks the egg). Serve topped with scallions, tamari or soy sauce, and pepper to taste.

Note: Dashi stock is sold in powder or concentrate form in many supermarkets and Asian stores. However, it's easy and nicer to make your own (the ingredients are sold in the same shops). Put a sheet of kombu seaweed about 2 inches square in a saucepan with 4 cups cold water. Bring slowly to a boil over a gentle heat. Just before boiling, remove the kombu. Stir in 1 oz. grated dried bonito, turn off the heat, and let cool. When the bonito has settled to the bottom, skim off any foam, then strain the stock and use. The kombu and bonito can be used to make a second batch. The stock will keep in the fridge for 3 days, or can be frozen. (Kombu is often toasted first by waving it briefly over a gas flame or heating it for about 30 seconds under a hot broiler.)

4 fresh corn cobs or about 2 cups fresh corn kernels
4 cups hot dashi stock* or chicken stock

To serve, your choice of:
4 egg yolks (optional)
4 scallions, sliced diagonally
2 tablespoons tamari or dark soy sauce
**cracked black pepper, or a Japanese pepper mixture
    such as furikake seasoning or seven-spice**

serves 4

A variation on a traditional Japanese summer soup, prized for the fresh taste of corn—and very easy to make.

A few dried porcini mushrooms will give a stronger mushroom flavor to a soup made with ordinary cultivated mushrooms. Use large, open-cap field mushrooms to give a deeper color.

Put the dried porcini in a bowl, add 1 cup boiling water and let soak for about 15 minutes. Heat the oil in a skillet, add the fresh mushrooms and sauté until colored but still firm.

Add the onion to the skillet, sauté until softened, then add the garlic, nutmeg, and parsley. Rinse any grit out of the porcini and strain their soaking liquid several times through cheesecloth. Add the liquid and porcini to the skillet (reserve a few small ones for garnish). Bring to a boil, then transfer to a blender. Reserve a few of the sautéed mushrooms for garnish and add the remaining mushroom mixture to the blender. Add 2 ladles of chicken stock, then blend to a purée.

Heat the butter in a saucepan, stir in the flour and cook gently, stirring continuously, until the mixture is very dark brown (take care or it will burn). Add the remaining stock, 1 ladle at a time, stirring well after each addition. Add the puréed mushroom mixture, bring to a boil, then simmer for 20 minutes. Add salt and pepper to taste, then serve topped with a few reserved mushrooms, coarsely chopped parsley, and a dollop of cream.

1 oz. dried porcini mushrooms

$\frac{1}{4}$ cup olive oil

6 large, open-capped field mushrooms, wiped, trimmed, and sliced

1 onion, halved and finely sliced

3 garlic cloves, crushed

a pinch of freshly grated nutmeg

leaves from a large bunch of parsley, finely chopped in a food processor

5 cups boiling chicken stock

$\frac{1}{4}$ cup butter

$\frac{1}{4}$ cup flour

sea salt and freshly ground black pepper

To serve:

$\frac{1}{4}$–$\frac{1}{3}$ cup coarsely chopped parsley

$\frac{1}{4}$–$\frac{1}{3}$ cup light cream

serves 4–6

italian mushroom soup

with porcini and parsley

cream of broccoli soup

with leeks and fava beans

A pale green, fresh, summery soup that can be adapted to other ingredients—it's also good with cauliflower and cannellini beans.

Heat the butter and oil in a large saucepan, add the leeks and sauté gently until softened but not browned. Reserve a few spoonfuls of the cooked leeks for garnish.

Add the broccoli to the pan and stir-fry until bright green. Add the potato, stock, and 4 cups water and bring to a boil. Reduce the heat, add salt and pepper and simmer for 30 minutes.

Pop the cooked fava beans out of their gray skins and discard the skins. Reserve a few spoonfuls of fava beans for garnish.

Strain the soup into a bowl and put the solids and the fava beans in a blender. Add 2 ladles of the strained liquid and purée until smooth. Add the remaining liquid and blend again. Reheat the soup, pour into heated soup bowls, top with the reserved leeks and skinned fava beans, then serve.

2 tablespoons butter

2 tablespoons corn or sunflower oil

2 large leeks, chopped

1 head broccoli, broken into florets

1 potato, cut into chunks

2½ cups vegetable or chicken stock

sea salt and freshly ground black pepper

1 cup shelled, cooked fava beans

serves 4–6

A favorite soup in the Antipodes, usually made with boiled pumpkin, but I rather like the smoky taste of this baked variety. A sprinkle of freshly ground nutmeg can be added at the end.

2 lb. pumpkin, cut into wedges

sunflower or corn oil, for roasting and sautéing

4 cups chicken stock

2 large potatoes, cut into chunks

salt and freshly ground black pepper

1 cup milk

¼ cup sour cream, to serve

serves 4

pumpkin soup

To make pumpkin crisps, cut about 20 fine slices off one of the wedges of pumpkin with a vegetable peeler, so you get an edge of green skin. Set aside.

Peel and seed the remaining pumpkin and cut into large chunks. Brush a baking tray with oil, add the pumpkin chunks, and brush them with oil too. Put in a preheated oven at 400°F and cook until browned outside and soft and fluffy inside, about 30 minutes, according to the size of the chunks.

Meanwhile, bring the chicken stock to a boil, add the potatoes and cook for about 20 minutes until soft. Put the potatoes into a blender and reserve the stock.

Pour about 1 inch depth of oil into a wok and heat until a piece of bread browns in 30 seconds. Add the fine slices of pumpkin and deep-fry until crispy. Remove and drain on crumpled paper towels.

Add the roasted pumpkin to the blender, add seasoning, milk, and a ladle of hot stock. Purée until smooth and creamy, adding more stock if necessary. (You may have to work in batches, according to the size of your blender.)

Transfer to a clean saucepan, season to taste, and reheat to just below boiling point. Ladle into heated soup bowls, top with a swirl of sour cream and a few pumpkin crisps, and serve with crusty bread.

mexican salsa soup

1 fresh corn cob

2 tablespoons sunflower or corn oil

½ onion, diced

1 yellow bell pepper, peeled and sliced

1 red bell pepper, peeled and sliced

2 red tomatoes, peeled and seeded

1 tablespoon fresh thyme leaves

1 tablespoon fresh oregano leaves

sea salt and freshly ground black pepper

1 basket yellow cherry tomatoes, halved, to serve (optional)

serves 4

Put the corn, blunt end down, on a board and shave off the kernels with a sharp knife. Put the oil and kernels in a saucepan and stir-fry gently for about 5 minutes. Remove from the heat.

Put all the remaining ingredients (except the yellow tomatoes) in a food processor and pulse briefly until chopped but still chunky

Add to the pan then cook gently for 6–8 minutes. Serve topped with halved yellow cherry tomatoes.

Everyone likes a spicy Mexican salsa. This is my favorite, turned into a soup—make it in a food processor for a coarser texture. Cut the peppers in half and peel with a vegetable peeler.

This very simple soup is packed with taste, thanks to the blended flavorings. Don't worry if you don't have all of them—onion, garlic, and ginger are the most important. If you don't have tamarind paste, stir in a squeeze of lime juice instead.

FISH AND SEAFOOD

To make the spice paste, put the lemongrass, lime leaves or zest, onion, garlic, and ginger in a blender and purée until smooth.

Put the stock in a saucepan, add the tomatoes and spice paste, and bring to a boil. Simmer for 5–10 minutes. Add the fish and fish sauce or soy. Poach for 5 minutes until opaque (do not let boil).

Put the pieces of fish and tomatoes in large soup bowls, stir the tamarind paste into the stock, return to a boil, then ladle over the fish. Serve topped with sprigs of cilantro.

asian fish soup

with ginger and tomatoes

Spice paste:

1 stalk lemongrass, finely sliced

2 kaffir lime leaves, very finely sliced, or a curl of lime zest

1 onion, finely sliced

3 garlic cloves, crushed

1 inch fresh ginger, finely chopped

6 cups fish stock

6 tomatoes, peeled and seeded

2 lb. thick white fish fillets, such as cod or haddock, cut in thick slices

1 tablespoon fish sauce or soy sauce

1 tablespoon smooth tamarind paste (see opposite)

sprigs of cilantro, to serve

serves 4–6

provençal fish soup with rouille

To make the rouille, put the bread in a bowl, sprinkle with about 1 tablespoon water, squeeze together, then squeeze dry. Put the egg yolk, garlic, chilies, and bread in a blender and purée until smooth. With the motor running, gradually add enough olive oil to make a thick paste. (If you're concerned about raw egg, omit it.)

Clean all the fish and seafood and cut the large pieces of fish into chunks. Put the mussels or clams, if using, in a large saucepan with 1 tablespoon water, cover, and heat until they open, shaking the pan from time to time. Remove and set aside as they open.

Heat the oil in a large, deep skillet, add the onion and leek, if using, and cook until softened and translucent. Add the tomatoes, garlic, bay leaves, and saffron. Simmer for 10 minutes. Add the fish, seafood, and water or stock, bring to a boil, reduce the heat, and simmer until the fish is opaque, about 2–3 minutes. Season to taste with salt and pepper

Divide the fish and seafood between large bowls, then ladle in the liquid. Serve the toast, rouille, and grated cheese separately.

To eat, spread the slices of toasted baguette with rouille, add to the soup, and sprinkle with grated cheese.

Rouille:

2 thick slices fresh French-style bread

1 egg yolk (see method)

3 garlic cloves, crushed

2 dried red chilies, seeded and crushed

olive oil (see method)

2 lb. assorted fish fillets and seafood

12–20 mussels and/or clams (optional)

½ cup extra-virgin olive oil

1 onion, sliced

1 large leek, sliced (optional)

3 large tomatoes, peeled and chopped

3 large garlic cloves, crushed

3 small fresh bay leaves

1 sachet saffron powder

4 cups water or fish stock

sea salt and freshly ground black pepper

To serve:

1 small bowl grated cheese, such as Gruyère

1 baguette, sliced diagonally and toasted

serves 4

Rouille, the peppery Provençal sauce, is the blended element of this soup. Delicious with many dishes, it is traditional with fish soup.

A bisque is a soup made with shellfish like shrimp, crabs, or lobster —a blender or food processor is the easiest way to make it. If fresh shrimp are too expensive, Chinese dried shrimp have great flavor.

Put the dried shrimp and saffron threads, if using, in a small bowl and cover with boiling water. Set aside until the shrimp soften.

Heat the oil in a large, heavy-based saucepan, add the shallots and sauté until softened and translucent. Add the garlic and shrimp shells and stir-fry until aromatic. Add the stock, bay leaf, dried shrimp and saffron, and their soaking liquid. Boil hard for about 5 minutes so the stock and oil amalgamate. Add the harissa, fish, and shrimp and poach for 5 minutes until the fish is opaque.

Remove the bay leaf, strain the soup into a bowl or pitcher, and transfer the solids, including the shells, to a blender. Add 1–2 ladles stock and blend until smooth. Push the mixture through a strainer into the rinsed saucepan, then transfer the solids back into the blender. Add more stock, blend again, and push through a strainer again. Repeat until all the stock has been used. The more you blend and push, the stronger the flavor will be.

Discard the solids in the strainer and reheat the soup in the saucepan. Stir in the lemon juice and salt to taste, then serve. The toast and rouille (page 36) would also be delicious with this soup.

1 package Chinese dried shrimp (about 2 oz.)

a large pinch of saffron threads or 1 sachet saffron powder

2 tablespoons olive oil

2 large shallots, chopped

2 garlic cloves, crushed

2 lb. shrimp, cooked or uncooked, shells reserved, or 1 extra package dried shrimp

4 cups fish stock

1 bay leaf

2 tablespoons harissa paste

2 lb. fish fillets, such as snapper or redfish

juice of ½ lemon

sea salt

serves 4

shrimp bisque

Jerusalem artichokes are potato-like root vegetables native to North America—now hugely popular around the world. They have a wonderful, elegant flavor: try them—you'll love them.

Boil the artichokes until tender. Drain, cool a little, then peel. Discard the skins and cooking water. Put the stock in a large saucepan, add the fish, bring to a boil, then turn off the heat and leave for 5 minutes. Transfer the fish to a plate, remove and discard the skin and bones, break the flesh into large pieces, cover, and keep it warm. Reserve the stock in the saucepan.

Heat the oil in a skillet, add the bacon and cook until crisp. Remove the bacon and drain on paper towels. Add the butter to the skillet, add the leek and sauté until translucent (do not let brown). Add the garlic and sauté for 1 minute. Transfer to the saucepan, add the artichokes, potatoes, herbs, seasoning, and water to cover. Simmer for 20 minutes. Remove the herbs, add the milk, transfer to a blender, and purée until smooth, adding extra boiling water if the mixture is too thick. Put the fish in heated soup bowls, ladle in the chowder, and serve topped with bacon and thyme or bay leaf.

1 lb. Jerusalem artichokes, unpeeled

1¼ cups fish or chicken stock

about 1 lb. smoked fish, such as haddock

1 tablespoon olive oil

2 slices smoked bacon, cut crosswise
   into 1-inch pieces

1 tablespoon butter

1 leek, white only, finely sliced

1 garlic clove, crushed

2 potatoes, finely sliced

1 bay leaf

2 sprigs of thyme

sea salt and freshly ground black pepper

1¼ cups hot milk

serves 4

jerusalem artichoke chowder

with smoked haddock and crispy bacon

The blended element of this soup is the red curry paste. Make in bulk, then freeze in ice cube trays. Asian soups are quick and easy to make if you have the spice pastes on hand.

MEAT AND POULTRY

To make the curry paste, remove the seeds from the chilies if preferred. Stir-fry the coriander and cumin seeds in a dry skillet for 2 minutes to release the aromas. Let cool. Put all the paste ingredients in a blender and purée in bursts. Use 2–4 tablespoons for this recipe and freeze the remainder.

Soak the rice stick noodles, if using, in hot water for 15 minutes. Boil for 1–2 minutes, then drain and plunge into cold water.

Put the stock in a saucepan, add 2–4 tablespoons of the curry paste and bring to a boil. Add the eggplants, if using, and the beans. Return to a boil, simmer for 15 minutes, then stir in the fish sauce or salt and sugar. Drain the noodles, cover with boiling water, then drain again.

Divide noodles and vegetables between large bowls. Add the beef, ladle in boiling stock (which instantly cooks the beef), and serve.

thai spicy beef soup

Red Thai curry paste:

5–10 dried red chilies, soaked in hot water for 30 minutes, then drained

½ teaspoon coriander seeds

½ teaspoon cumin seeds

separated cloves from 1 whole garlic bulb

2–3 pink Thai shallots or 1 regular

1 inch fresh ginger, finely sliced

grated zest of 1 lime, preferably a kaffir lime

1 teaspoon sea salt

1 tablespoon fish sauce

6 oz. dried wide rice stick noodles (optional)

2 cups chicken or beef stock

3 egg-shaped white or yellow eggplants, quartered and seeded (optional)

6 Chinese long beans, cut into 1-inch lengths

2 tablespoons fish sauce or a pinch of salt

1 teaspoon sugar

4 oz. beef fillet, frozen, then very finely sliced

serves 4

Delicious wonton fillings take seconds to make in a food processor.

wonton chicken soup

8 Chinese cabbage leaves

1 poached chicken breast, shredded

1 carrot, finely sliced lengthwise, blanched

2 scallions, finely sliced lengthwise

a handful of fresh bean sprouts, trimmed

Wontons:

4 oz. pork fillet or chicken breast, sliced

3 scallions, chopped

a pinch of salt

1 teaspoon grated fresh ginger

2 water chestnuts, chopped

12 small wonton skins

1 egg white, lightly beaten with a fork

Chinese chicken stock:

6 cups chicken stock

4 whole star anise

2 inches fresh ginger, peeled and sliced

1 onion, sliced

salt, to taste

serves 4

Bring a large saucepan of water to a boil. Add the Chinese cabbage leaves and blanch for 1 minute. Plunge into a bowl of ice water for 5 minutes. Drain. Cut out and discard the white ribs. Put 4 leaves, one on top of the other, on a kitchen towel. Roll them up into a cylinder and press out the liquid. Cut the cylinder crosswise into 1-inch long sections. Repeat with the other 4 leaves.

To make the wontons, put the pork or chicken in a food processor and pulse until ground. Add the scallions, salt, and ginger and pulse again. Transfer to a bowl and stir in the water chestnuts. Brush a circle of egg white around the center of each wonton skin and put 1 teaspoon of mixture in the middle. Twirl the wonton skin around the filling to make a shuttlecock shape. Press to seal.

Put the stock ingredients in a saucepan and simmer for 10 minutes. Cool, strain, then strain through cheesecloth at least 4 times to clarify the stock. Reheat, then poach the wontons for 1½ minutes. Divide the wontons, stock, chicken, cabbage, and carrot between heated soup plates and top with the scallions and bean sprouts.

coconut laksa

with chicken and noodles

Spice paste:

3–6 red or orange chilies, cored and chopped

1 shallot, chopped

2 stalks lemongrass, finely sliced

1 inch fresh ginger, finely sliced

½ teaspoon ground turmeric

6 blanched almonds, chopped

1 tablespoon fish sauce or a pinch of salt

1 garlic clove, crushed

3 tablespoons peanut oil

2 cups canned coconut milk

2 boneless chicken breasts, skinned and
   thickly sliced

fish sauce or salt, to taste

1½ lb. fresh or 4 oz. dried udon noodles

To serve:

1 package bean sprouts, rinsed and trimmed

4 scallions, sliced diagonally

1 red chili, cored and finely sliced

sprigs of fresh cilantro (optional)

serves 4

Spice pastes are usually laboriously made with a mortar and pestle—a blender is an easy, modern alternative.

Put all the spice paste ingredients into a blender and work to a paste (add a little water if necessary).

Heat the oil in a wok, add the spice paste and cook gently for about 5 minutes. Add 4 cups boiling water, then the coconut milk, bring to a boil, stirring, then add the chicken and return to a boil. Reduce to a simmer and poach the chicken for 10–15 minutes or until cooked through. Add fish sauce or salt, to taste.

If using fresh noodles, rinse in cold water, then boil for about 1–2 minutes. If using dried noodles, cook in boiling unsalted water for 10–12 minutes, then drain. Divide the noodles between large soup bowls. Add the chicken and liquid, top with the bean sprouts, scallions, chili, and cilantro, if using, and serve.

tomato and bean soup

with spicy harissa paste

A very quick and comforting soup on a cold winter night—a food processor will give a coarser, more interesting texture than a blender.

Put the tomatoes, beans, and stock in a food processor, in batches if necessary, and pulse briefly until coarsely chopped but not smooth. Transfer to a saucepan, add the crushed garlic, lemon juice, and harissa paste and heat to just below boiling, stirring. Thin with boiling water, if necessary. Season, then serve.

Variation: serve sprinkled with chopped parsley, snipped chives, grated Parmesan cheese, and crusty bread on the side.

2 cups crushed Italian tomatoes

2 cups cooked red kidney beans

2 cups chicken stock

2 garlic cloves, crushed

juice of 1 large lemon

2 tablespoons harissa paste or chili paste

salt

serves 4–6

Many supermarkets sell fresh ready-shelled peas, so this recipe can be made easily. If you cook the peas in a microwave, in the package, with little or no liquid, their flavor will be concentrated.

To cook the peas, microwave on HIGH for 3–4 minutes, or follow the package instructions. Alternatively, simmer in boiling water with a pinch of salt for about 2–3 minutes or until tender.

Meanwhile, heat the olive oil in a skillet, add the pancetta, and sauté until crispy. Remove and drain on crumpled paper towels.

Put the peas in a blender with 1–2 ladles boiling stock. Work to a purée, adding extra stock if necessary. Add the remaining stock and blend again. Taste and adjust the seasoning. Reheat, thinning with a little boiling water if necessary, then ladle into heated soup bowls and serve, topped with crispy bacon and sprigs of mint.

1 lb. shelled peas (about 3 packs)
4 cups boiling chicken stock
sea salt and freshly ground black pepper

To serve:
1 tablespoon olive oil
8 slices pancetta or bacon, quartered
sprigs of mint

serves 4

fresh pea soup

with mint and crispy bacon

lebanese chickpea soup

with cream, pepper, and parsley

4 cups boiling chicken stock

2 cups hummus, ready-made or
   homemade

Homemade hummus (optional):

2 cups cooked or canned chickpeas
   (garbanzos), drained if canned

2 tablespoons olive oil

1 onion, chopped

3 garlic cloves, crushed

sea salt and freshly ground black pepper

chicken or vegetable stock (see method)

To serve:

¼ cup cream

cracked black pepper

a handful of parsley leaves (optional)

serves 4

This soup version of hummus is creamy and delicious. I include a recipe for homemade hummus, but you can also use the store-bought variety if you're in a hurry.

If making your own hummus, put all the ingredients except the stock in a blender and work to a smooth purée. Thin with stock to form a thick, spreadable consistency. Use 2 cups for the soup and reserve the rest for another use.

Put the hummus in the blender, add 1 ladle of the boiling chicken stock, and purée. Add the remaining stock and blend again. Reheat if necessary, then serve, topped with a trail of cream, cracked pepper, and a few parsley leaves, if using.

jamaican bean soup with chilies

1½ cups dried red beans, such as rose coco,
rose cowpeas, or red kidney beans

2 large onions, 1 quartered, 1 cut into
wedges to make petals, then separated

3 large garlic cloves, crushed

3 tablespoons olive oil

6 slices smoked bacon, coarsely chopped

1 baking potato, chopped

1 habanero chili, pricked several times
with a toothpick

1 large sprig of thyme

3 cups chicken stock or water

sea salt and freshly ground black pepper

To serve (optional):

crispy bacon

thyme leaves

serves 4

Put the beans in a measuring cup and add 2½ cups boiling water. Soak for a few hours or overnight. Drain and rinse.

Put in a saucepan with water to cover, bring to a boil, then boil hard for 10 minutes. Drain, return to the pan, add 3 cups cold water, the quartered onion, and 1 garlic clove. Bring to a boil and simmer for about 30 minutes or until the beans are tender. Drain.

Heat the oil in a stockpot or saucepan, add the bacon and sliced onion and cook until softened and translucent. Add the potato and the remaining garlic and cook until golden. Add the chili, thyme, beans, and stock, with salt and pepper to taste. Bring to a boil, simmer gently for 15–30 minutes, then remove the thyme and chili. If serving the chili, seed it and finely slice the flesh.

Put the beans, vegetables, and cooking liquid in a blender and purée until smooth, in batches if necessary. Divide between heated soup plates. Serve, topped with crispy bacon, thyme leaves, or the finely sliced chili, if using.

In Jamaica, when a girl marries, her stockpot is the first thing she needs to set up house. It is the perfect pot for this soup, but if you don't have one, an ordinary heavy-based saucepan will have to do.

creamy french almond soup

This sumptuous soup is loosely based on the classic French Onion Soup. The broth is thickened with almond milk—a delicious alternative to cream and perfect for people who "don't do dairy."

2 tablespoons olive oil

2 large onions, sliced

2 garlic cloves, crushed

½ cup white wine (optional)

4 cups boiling chicken or vegetable stock

1½ cups shelled almonds

1 baguette, finely sliced, then oven-toasted until golden

4 oz. Gruyère cheese or cheddar, grated into long strips

sea salt and freshly ground black pepper

serves 4

Heat the oil in a large, heavy-based saucepan, add the onion and sauté until softened and golden. Add the garlic and sauté for about 1 minute until golden. Add the wine, if using, and boil hard until reduced to 2 tablespoons. Add the stock and boil for 2 minutes.

Put the almonds in a blender or food processor and grind to a fine meal. Add half the wine-stock mixture and blend well. Pass through a fine strainer back into the saucepan, pressing through as much almond milk as possible. Return the nuts to the blender, add another 2–3 ladles of the liquid from the pan. Repeat, blending and straining, at least twice more, to extract as much almond milk as possible from the nuts. Add the almond milk to the remaining wine-stock mixture and season to taste.

Divide the soup between ovenproof bowls, top with slices of toast and some cheese, and put under a hot broiler for 1–2 minutes until the cheese begins to melt. Serve with extra grated cheese.

indian yellow lentil soup

with mustard seed tempering

South Indians must have the most wonderful vegetarian food ever invented. They have been vegetarian for thousands of years and the many kinds of lentils, known as *dhaal*, provide protein in the diet.

Put the yellow lentils, turmeric, cumin, and chili in a saucepan, cover with 4 cups cold water, and bring to a boil. Simmer, covered, until tender (the time will depend on the age and variety). Purée in a blender, in batches if necessary. Transfer to a clean saucepan and stir in enough boiling stock to make a thick, soupy consistency. Reheat to just below boiling point, then taste and adjust the seasoning.

To make the tempering, heat the oil in a skillet, add the mustard and cardamom seeds, and stir-fry until they pop. Add the onion and cook until lightly browned. Add the garlic and chili, if using, and stir-fry for about 1 minute to release the aromas.

Serve the soup in bowls or cups, topped with a spoonful of tempering and a dollop of plain yogurt, if using.

1½ cups yellow lentils (channa dhaal) or
    yellow split peas
½ teaspoon ground turmeric
½ teaspoon cumin seeds
1 small red dried chili, seeded
boiling vegetable stock (see method)
¼ cup plain yogurt, to serve (optional)
salt

Mustard seed tempering:
3 tablespoons corn or mustard oil or ghee
1 tablespoon mustard seeds
1 tablespoon cardamom seeds
1 onion, halved and finely sliced lengthwise
2 fat garlic cloves, crushed
1 red chili, cored and finely sliced (optional)

serves 4

My Danish ancestors were great fans of fruit soups as an appetizer or dessert. I grew up in tropical Australia, and if any mangoes survived the greedy attention of children and cattle, we would have loved to make soup out of them. Alas, they never did!

Put the mango pulp in the blender with the ice, champagne, if using, the ginger purée, sliced stem ginger, and the ginger syrup and blend until smooth. Add enough ice water to produce the consistency of thin cream. Serve in chilled soup bowls or glasses and top with shreds of grated lime zest.

Notes: To purée fresh (ripe) mangoes, put the flesh in a blender with the juice of 1 lime or lemon. Blend until smooth. About 4 large mangoes produce 2 cups.
To make ginger purée, break fresh ginger into pieces and soak in water for 1 hour. Drain, peel, and slice, then blend with a little lemon juice or water until smooth. Freeze in ice cube trays and use when needed.

2 cups mango pulp, canned or fresh*
1 cup crushed ice
1 cup demi-sec champagne or more ice
2 tablespoons ginger purée*
4 pieces preserved stem ginger, finely sliced
4 tablespoons of ginger syrup from the jar
grated zest of 2 limes

serves 4

chilled mango soup with champagne and ginger

watermelon soup with chili flakes

Sweet watermelon tastes amazing blended with the spicy prickle of dried chili flakes. Use the reddest, ripest melons you can find.

1 round, chilled, ripe watermelon, cut into wedges
1 tablespoon chili flakes, plus extra, to serve
ice cubes, to serve (optional)

serves 4

Cut the seedless parts out of the watermelon and put into the blender (reserve any juice).

Cut the seedy part out of each wedge and put it in a strainer set over a bowl. Press the flesh through the strainer (don't worry too much about getting it all), then transfer the contents of the bowl to the blender.

Blend, in batches if necessary, until smooth. Add the chili, blend briefly, then serve in chilled soup plates and add ice cubes, if using, and extra chili flakes.

melon soup with japanese pink pickled ginger

Use very scented melons, such as green honeydew or orange cantaloupe. Don't chill them, or you will deaden their flavor.

2 ripe cantaloupe- or honeydew-style melons
2 cups crushed ice
1 tablespoon ground ginger
1 tablespoon freshly cracked black pepper
2 tablespoons chopped Japanese pink pickled ginger
sprigs of mint or borage flowers (optional)
ice cubes, to serve

serves 4

Halve and seed the melons. Using a spoon, scoop out the flesh into a blender or food processor. Add the ice and ground ginger and work, in bursts, to a purée. Add enough ice water to make a pourable consistency.

Serve in bowls with ice cubes, pepper, pink pickled ginger, and mint leaves or borage flowers, if using.

conversion chart

Weights and measures have been rounded
up or down slightly to make measuring easier.

volume equivalents:

american	metric	imperial	
1 teaspoon	5 ml		
1 tablespoon	15 ml		
¼ cup	60 ml	2 fl.oz.	
⅓ cup	75 ml	2½ fl.oz.	
½ cup	125 ml	4 fl.oz.	
⅔ cup	150 ml	5 fl.oz.	(¼ pint)
¾ cup	175 ml	6 fl.oz.	
1 cup	250 ml	8 fl.oz.	

weight equivalents: measurements:

imperial	metric	inches	cm
1 oz.	25 g	¼ inch	5 mm
2 oz.	50 g	½ inch	1 cm
3 oz.	75 g	¾ inch	1.5 cm
4 oz.	125 g	1 inch	2.5 cm
5 oz.	150 g	2 inches	5 cm
6 oz.	175 g	3 inches	7 cm
7 oz.	200 g	4 inches	10 cm
8 oz.	250 g	5 inches	12 cm
9 oz.	275 g	6 inches	15 cm
10 oz.	300 g	7 inches	18 cm
11 oz.	325 g	8 inches	20 cm
12 oz.	375 g	9 inches	23 cm
13 oz.	400 g	10 inches	25 cm
14 oz.	425 g	11 inches	28 cm
15 oz.	475 g	12 inches	30 cm
16 oz. (1 lb.)	500 g		
2 lb.	1 kg		

oven temperatures:

225°F	110°C	Gas ¼
250°F	120°C	Gas ½
275°F	140°C	Gas 1
300°F	150°C	Gas 2
325°F	160°C	Gas 3
350°F	180°C	Gas 4
375°F	190°C	Gas 5
400°F	200°C	Gas 6
425°F	220°C	Gas 7
450°F	230°C	Gas 8
475°F	240°C	Gas 9